Pedestrian Traffic

poems by

Carla Criscuolo

Finishing Line Press
Georgetown, Kentucky

Pedestrian Traffic

ACKNOWLEDGMENTS

I would like to thank the editors of the following literary magazines for giving earlier
versions of these poems a home:

Chantarelle's Notebook – "Retention" and "The Appraisal"
decomp – "Witness"
disenthralled – "Morpheme"
Foliate Oak – "Serenade"
Lunarosity – "Rapacity" and "Twister"
Main Channel Voices – "Not a Poet"
Main Street Rag – "Posing"
South Jersey Underground – "Use Once and Destroy"

I would also like to thank all the people and places that have provided me with artistic,
emotional, physical, and financial support through the years: Mom, Dad, Michael and the
rest of the fam, Gemma Billings, Tina Browder, Beth Ann Fennelly, Heather Frankland,
Knox College, Matthew Lindquist, Gregory Miller, New York City, Dolores Pacileo,
Elisabeth Pacileo, Gayle Perez, Elizabeth Seidel, Betsy Sholl, Leslie Ullman, Vermont
College of Fine Arts, Jay Wartenberg, and David Wojahn.

Editor: Christen Kincaid

Cover Art: Carla Criscuolo

Author Photo: Carla Criscuolo

Cover Design: Elizabeth Maines

Printed in the USA on acid-free paper.
Order online: www.finishinglinepress.com
              also available on amazon.com

Author inquiries and mail orders:
Finishing Line Press
P. O. Box 1626
Georgetown, Kentucky 40324
U. S. A.

Table of Contents

For my father,
Lou Criscuolo

Montana

The train attendant knocks on the door to my
sleeping car. "What time would you like to proceed
to the dining car for supper?" I'll skip it, I tell him.
If I wanted to converse with the locals I'd get off
at the next station, ask the first hick in overalls
to tell me about his cattle ranch. I never knew

there were large swaths of America that look
like a John Wayne film, a few thousand years of
wind erosion and sediment staring back at you
from every summit in Montana. There are bright fields

of sunflowers, blooms all facing East, nothing but
uninhabited land reaching all the way to the horizon,
blanketed by a sky so low you could reach up,
and touch the clouds. In New York City,

space is a commodity you pay thousands to enjoy.
Out here there is so much, I could build a hundred
New Yorks for every station stop. I write that down,
one hundred New Yorks.

The train attendant knocks again. "Sure you don't
want dinner? It's included in the cost of your ticket."
Let him think I'm asleep. People do not resonate
the way a beautiful view does, its stoic

grandeur something to be absorbed, polished,
displayed during dinner parties. I am gathering
the words to describe it. Already fashioning
the tale of my marauder self.

Taxi Cab Nativity

The rustle of tourists shuffling through Times Square,
the shriek of sirens echoing down every street, the thump
of drum sticks on overturned buckets ricocheting off trees
in Central Park. I was born in the middle of all this sound.
Felt it fuse to my central nervous system, each vibration
thrum up my spine, electrifying every skin cell and
hair follicle until my body shone like a Broadway marquee
plugged into the sun. Can't isolate the tones any more than
I can peel the arteries from my arms. My lungs fill themselves
with songs made of soot and steam. The notes, off- key
and not, enter my blood stream, amplifying my cries until
there's nothing but the voice of God coming from my mouth.

Posing

Grandma pulls my whole costume
right out of the closet all the way
in the back of the apartment, where
mommy and daddy keep their
skis and suitcases.

She comes out with a little pink leotard,
pink tights, and pink ballet slippers
left from when she used to teach.
I wish grandma still danced,
then I could take lessons
on how to be like her when I grow up.

She helps me get dressed and we go
to show mommy how pretty I look.
Mommy puts a pink satin mask over
my eyes, and ties a pink scarf
around my waist. I spin in
circles and watch it float around my legs.

My big brother Michael is wearing a jacket
with green blotches on it, baggy black pants,
and a pair of sunglasses. He is carrying
an army-colored toy gun, like G. I. Joe.

Mommy stands me in front of the door.
She waves Michael next to me,
picks up her camera, and tells us to pose.
I don't remember any of the ballet poses
grandma showed me, so I just stand
with my hands behind my back.

Mommy tells us to do something interesting.
Michael throws his arm around my neck.
As I laugh, he pulls me to his side,
and puts his gun to my head.
Mommy snaps the picture.

Inertia

This bed is not a real bed, but
my parents pull out couch
whose lumpy cushions I have been
stuffing with dreams since
I relinquished my crib.

The check on the coffee table
is not my money. It is my father's
latest attempt to squeeze
some success out of me,
hoping to see it trickle
into a glass he can serve
to his friends.

He does not know
how quickly the waves
swell in my head or
how loudly they crash when
I sit down in front of the computer,
and watch all the letters lose their
sense. How they silence seagulls,
knock birds out of the sky
and onto the sand with
a mind-numbing thud.

I watch the dawn pull
her pink canopy across the sky,
listen as she wakes a roar
out of the city with each cup of
coffee sold, each retail manager
rolling up the security gate
on a storefront, every taxi cab
stalled in traffic. I want to respond

but the sound gets drowned out
by this haunting paralysis I cannot
seem to exorcise no matter
how many checks we stuff
into the pockets of the State
University, no matter how

many un-timed tests I am allowed
to take, no matter how many
job applications I fill out and
fail to return. No matter how much
I try to roar back, all that comes
out is a whimper.

Use Once and Destroy

His scalp gleams like the tunnel
walls when the 1 Train rolls
into the 14th Street subway station,
headlights turning decades
of grime all bright and reflective.
I keep my eyes on his receding
hairline so they won't wander
past his shoulder, down the length
of his arm, and over the restless
hand stroking up and down
the lengthening bulge in his pants.

He keeps his eyes covered,
the index and middle fingers
of his right hand spread
to reveal one bespectacled pupil,
blazing with hunger and
embarrassment, aimed directly at
me. I shift my gaze to the window
behind his head, pretend
to be fascinated by the sticker
above the window frame that's
supposed to say, *This is
an air-conditioned car. Please
close windows*. Someone has
replaced it with a sticker that says,
*This is a karma-conditioned car.
Please watch what you do.*
I wonder if he saw it before
he decided to sit across from me.

Empty orange and yellow
molded seats that would feel
at home in any MacDonalds
flank emergency exits
stuck with signs reminding
riders it is prohibited to move

between cars unless directed
by a police officer. There
is nothing to stop me from
accepting the invitation of
the next car, prohibitions
be damned! But moving
would mean admitting this man
has turned me into an object, a fetish,
a means to an end. I don't want
to believe in the jerking
motion of his wrist or
the gentle trembling
in my hands like a tea cup
responding to the approach
of a freight train.

I want to believe in
the homeless man with
gnarled teeth who pan handles
outside the 86th Street subway
entrance every morning,
always asking me for a smile
instead of a dime because
he knows my pockets are
as empty as his. I want
to believe in the GQ centerfold
who stepped onto the train
one night with a hand full of
daisies and walked the length
of the car offering one to each
and every woman; who knelt
before my drooping eyes and
slumped shoulders, grinned
like he was looking up into
a miracle, held out his hand
and asked, "Flower?"

I want to believe I am safe.

The train picks up
passengers at 18th and he doesn't
stop. The train picks up passengers
at 23rd and he doesn't stop. The train
picks up passengers at 28th
and they don't stop him,
so I fiddle with the cassette
in my walkman because
I'm sick of listening to
The Pixies and could really use
a dose of Public Enemy.

When we reach 42nd Street
he gets up, heads for
the sliding doors to my right,
turning his body sideways, pressing
himself against me as if trying
to squeeze past some obstruction
even though there isn't anything
blocking the exit; no baby
carriage the size of a tank
or buzzing hive of Catholic school
girls to maneuver past.

The apex of his crotch
nudges my arm, and the way
my stomach plummets
you'd think I was in the belly of
a descending airplane,
body going hollow
with the visceral realization
that there is so much room to fall
and no one to catch me. I startle
and gasp and whip my head around,

but he has disappeared onto
the writhing platform of three
piece suits and pencil skirts,
leaving my outrage with no place
to land. As the doors close, I see
a piece of paper glued flat against
the highest point of the station's
arched ceiling. It reads:
Birth Paint Death Cost.

The Guardian

You buzz through the night high on fumes and full
of calamity, a seventh beer in your fist, the sixth
burbling around in your stomach with a couple of
fuzzy navels and a glass of shiraz. Your eyes follow
the subtle sway of her hips as she smoothes out
the wrinkles in her skirt, notice her bare shoulders,
relaxed and loose as the pants of all those frat boys
who keep approaching her, their hands stashed
in pockets, white Polo shirts turned red by the strobe light,
flashing smiles that make their mouths drip with blood.

She has no idea how fierce your arrogance becomes
or how deliberate your speech when coupled with
inebriation. How that quote about free will you attribute
to Hobbes only slides from your mouth when you're
looking for a bolt to screw your passion into
for the night. When you start toward her I see my own
history unfolding, remember your tongue filling my mouth
like a sponge, sucking me limp, hands grasping
every curve. I remember how you dangled

the carrot of commitment before my eyes just to watch me
come running, and how I found you arched over the naked body
of another girl, one whose thighs had not yet achieved
the tremble brought on by too many nights of worthless
fucking. Someone has to be the rubber to your glue,
counteract the glistening lure of your tar-pit mouth, so I rise
and go to her, each step punctuated by heavy bass
shaking its way up through my legs, reminding me of
the way your body used to vibrate between them.

I walk up to her and ask how she is enjoying
the party, every cell in my body humming with
the awareness of your approach. I focus my eyes on hers,
use my back to shield her from yours, because I'd rather be
drenched in your hostility than allow you to speak
to her. I'd rather send you back to the bartender,
seething like prairie fire, feeling charred
when he tells you you're cut off.

Retention

I repeatedly print your name
across blank pieces of loose leaf
notebook paper, punishing myself
the way old schoolmarms once punished
misbehaving elementary school students.
The arch of each "m," the continuity of
each "o," and the sting of tendonitis remind me
of all the ways I asked the same question
hoping for a different answer; the question
put forth every time I scribbled hasty
notes just to say I was thinking of you
and wondering if you had read any
good books lately, the silent question that
accompanied every mix tape I sent to you
even though a twelve year old could
tell you what music compilations
and their labor mean, the question that
secured our secret firmly between
my legs in the shadow of the massive
field house where no one could see us.
My mother used to say there was no such thing
as a dumb question. I would add,
only if you do not already know the
answer. Your name is a question
I put to myself with the turn of each
full page. I want to know how
I got so wrapped up in these letters;
I want to know if there was an
"I" before you wrapped me in them.
I want to know how I can explain the loss
of something that may not have existed
at the time of the robbery, and if it is
robbery if you give something away
and then decide you want it back.
I dot and cross and punish myself
for asking stupid questions.

Morpheme

Pebbles slip off our tongues,
too small to cause even a ripple
in the silence that constricts us,
each sentence a futile offering,
weighing down on the next,
collapsing whatever lay
injected in our words.
We are paper dolls,
flat and featureless,
cut to perfection. We will throw
our tattered bodies to the wind
and hope the air will carry us.

Twister

We careen through sheets of rain
that pound the concrete like an angry
parent adding emphasis to a vital point,
siren screams chasing us down each block.
Vision obscured, tree limbs blowing
at right angles are periodically illuminated by
lightning bolts so strong they clear the clouds,
cast out the gathering grey in favor of
brilliant gold. Leigh runs ahead,

sopping hair plastered over her shoulders
like a cape. She knows violent weather,
became acquainted with it back in Nebraska
where spring brought nothing but broken windows
and storm cellers. I've no doubt my Bat Girl
will guide us through these deserted streets
unharmed. The black velvet skirt I got
for five dollars at the Salvation Army
sticks to my knees, rides up my thighs
exposing quivering, pale skin
unaccustomed to the brutality of
wind and rain after a winter spent hiding
under Lycra and denim. My boots

splash through puddles of mud,
my mouth unable to stay shut, my smile
shining a spotlight on Leigh's back
as we stampede across sidewalks
layered in worms, this approaching twister
giving my city-girl bones a taste of
mortality far more thrilling than the threat
of high school kids bringing guns to class
or jay walking across Queensborough
Boulevard. Not until we barrel

into the basement where the rest of our dorm
sits watching The Real World and pretending
to read Descartes will I realize that Leigh is
crying. I watch her drop to the floor,
breath coming in starts and stops, jerking
like a sixteen year old getting to know
the brake pedal, pull her knees up to her chest,
and sob in harmony with the howling wind.

Witness

The night she wore
that small stuffed toy llama
on her head to dinner,
front legs framing her face,
muzzle flopped forward
kissing her hairline,
an embarrassed friend asked,
"Why?" She said,
"Because I want to."
In those words I heard
the sound of a spark
jumping from the fire place
to the Persian rug,
of water boiling over
the side of a kettle,
the last Redbird subway
car pulling out of Flushing.
I wanted to be her,
all kinetic and unfettered.

I cannot imagine her
in bridal white, marching
down an aisle of mahogany
pews that end with
"Because I want to"
becoming
"Do you think I should?"
That day, I will stand
front and center
in a throng of bustling
girls aching for union.
When she tosses
life in the singular over
her shoulder, I will reach,
hoping the bouquet that
lands in my palm is still
warm from her grip.

Missing

There are nights the moon is invisible,
and no one notices. You'd think it would
be difficult to ignore an enormous navy blue
blanket suffocating the sky, but we do. Spend
so much time looking down, the sky loses
its wonder. All we see is asphalt, cement,
grass. All we think is *I hope I don't step in
dog shit*, and when we do, we berate
ourselves for not seeing it. How could we
be so stupid? It was right in front of us!
How did we miss it?

Serenade

I don't play songs for you anymore,
they go unnoticed, drowned out
by the thunderous sound of car horns
and taxi cab drivers cursing in Arabic,
the thumping bass line that shakes
your windowpanes, and the loud drunks
pissing in the alley next to
that trendy dance club beneath
your apartment. I could sing
a million love songs and you
wouldn't hear a word, ears
plugged by the ragged wail of
G. G. Allin coming through
your headphones. You've never
needed to hear love songs
the way I've needed to sing them,
in call and response fashion, crooning
a shy question, waiting for you to return
the notes and sentiment. I watch
the silhouette of your shoulders against
a drawn window shade - the gentle
tilt of your head as you look up to scan
the words on the computer screen,
the latest piece in the jigsaw puzzle
of your novel - and feel all the music
drain out of me, rush over the curb,
down Tenth Avenue and into the sewer drains.
I put one boot in front of the other, hoping
there is a subway entrance nearby so
all the late night merry makers can't
see me sulk through their fever pitched
night of lust and abandon. I would rather
go underground, monitor the rats as they
play at avoiding the third rail, wishing
I'd had the good sense to do the same.

The Appraisal

This would be so much easier if you'd just throw something
at me. Maybe that Lladro figurine your father gave you for your
eighth birthday—a ballerina tying up her pink pointe shoes, crouched
in a pose reminiscent of Rodin's "Thinker"—a treasure that has perched
atop every dresser your knit sweaters have ever graced from your childhood
bedroom with the gauzy white curtains and canopy bed, to our first
studio apartment above the bodega in Spanish Harlem where fat men in
straw hats sat out on the sidewalk playing poker and smoking cigars
all summer long. Do I mean that much to you? Could you bear to pitch
that satin and laced beauty at my face, watch her delicate weight crash and
shatter against the mantel just to show me what you really think of
the phrase I've been mumbling at my shoes for hours: *She meant nothing.*
I pictured an outburst, a banshee cry and your French tip fingernails
coming at my eyes. I pictured myself grabbing your wrists, restraining you,
holding you to my chest, and feeling your love for me shake your slim frame
into silent sobs. But this isn't what I imagined. I don't know how to
interpret your expressionless face, your dry eyes. Don't know how to weigh
this stoicism against my own betrayal, or what it means to pray for violence.

Pedestrian Traffic
For St. Mark's Place

The skateboarders at Astor Place are going to get us all
killed, launching Ollies and kickflips into oncoming traffic,
causing drivers to swerve and jump the curb, flipping
the finger to any motorist with the audacity to honk
at them. I dodge women in huge sunglasses with Starbucks
cups in one hand, cell phones in the other, Yorkies
straining against jewel studded leashes for a sniff
of my hand, gaggles of mothers pushing strollers
three astride, oblivious to the river of pedestrians
pounding against the dam of their backs. They are

superimposed over my memory of this street in 1995,
when tottering toothpicks in torn fishnets and Doc Martens
clomped up the stoop of the community center looking
for a fix. Leather clad squatters with green Mohawks
begged spare change outside the MacDonald's on
East Broadway, relying on the kindness of over funded
and under engaged NYU students when blow jobs were
no longer enough to scare up a dime bag. Gone are
the mountains of black garbage bags sprouting from the sidewalk
like dandelions. Gone are the fetish shops, front windows
full of leather chaps and brocade corsets, replaced by

the neon scream of a Quiznos sign. I can't even afford
to loiter outside Trash & Vaudeville, attempting to sniff out
any last remnants of my youth, inhaling nothing but
gentrification. But not even that can exterminate
the skate rats still smearing tag names on the Cube
in bright pastel letters that glow against the smooth
black surface. Still blind to any but their own
forward momentum.

Rapacity

Even after all my hairs have turned
grey and I have taken to wearing
button down sweaters in the spring
and walking down the promenade
in Riverside Park every afternoon
at three, smelling the tulips, posies,
the earthy scent of the Hudson, I won't
be able to tell you what you did to me.
Not even the protection of crow's feet
and faded memories could lend me
enough courage to look you in the eye,
explain the torture of sitting across
from you week after week, wanting
nothing but permission to crawl
across that massive conference table
and stroke your pale cheek, rub
my hands against the coarse stubble
of your chin as the professor pressed
her hand to her throat and looked
on in disbelief. How could I admit
to the torrential showers of want
that beaded my forehead whenever
you greeted me in the halls, a ravaging
smirk across your lips like you knew?
Neither then nor now could I be
so bold as to tell you that your kiss
had the power of every cliché behind it
and my knees never really regained
their strength after that night
behind the field house. You can't know that
all these years later I would still give
my heartbeat to steal away with you
to some shadowy corner where secrets
accumulate like karmic debt.
All we had was a once, but once
we had it, it was all I wanted.

You can't know that I must eat the lie
whenever your number appears
on my cell phone, a thousand sighs
and fluttery words about the latest
butterfly to make her way to your web;
elaborate descriptions of each perfect
wing, their sharp colors, oh yes,
this is the one. I wish I could tell them
about you and your taste for beauty
and innocence; about how many of us have
stumbled away from you only to
find ourselves stuck, laced into
a web of charm that makes the struggle
to escape even more delicious
than the prospect of freedom.

Work Study

This library should have
a dress code, something
to keep you from walking in
here wearing that skin tight
wife beater, cowboy hat,
and rakish smile. Seriously,
you should have to
check your hotness at the door
because it's making all
the librarians sweat. You tip
your hat and my brain turns
to TV snow. "Hey Boss," you whisper,
and I want to tell you to leave,
come back in, and say "Howdy"
instead. I want to ask you,
"What's with the necklace dude?
Conch shells? Really?
Did some hippie-chick from
Oregon get her hands on you?"
There's a splash of purple peeking
out from under those shells.
I see you see me see it,
and you flash a sheepish grin.
Show off.

Fade to Grey

You are exactly the kind of boy I would have
crushed on when I was eighteen, the kind of boy
who walks with the swagger of Jerry Cantrell
exuding an Eddie Vedder surliness. The kind
of boy that hunches thin Kurt Cobain shoulders
around his last cigarette and only washes
his hair once a week.

I cross my legs, sit up straight, make sure
the curve of my back is clearly visible,
lower my eyes, and wait for you to look up
from your coffee and Rolling Stone magazine
so I can glance up just then, hook you with
a shy smile, and reel you in. I tick off
the minutes, follow the soft click of the second
hand on my wrist watch, but when your head

finally bobs up, you are not looking at me.
You are looking at the two young women
across the street stepping out of American Eagle.
You are looking at curve-hugging tank tops
sloped over breasts that are still blossoming,
Daisy Dukes showing off Katy Perry legs,
laughter like church bells in full gong.

I am suddenly very aware that I am dressed
in jeans that come up to my waist, and a pair of
very sensible Rockports. Strands of hair are
falling from my ponytail, tickling my nose,
and there is nothing sexy about this button-
down sweater bought on clearance at Chico's.

There is a man sitting at the table next to mine,
so close I can smell his espresso. There is a bald spot
just starting to form at his crown. He wears
Tevas and cargo shorts, a bit of flab pushing up
against his Slayer t-shirt. It must have been black
at one time, years and wash cycles having turned it
a soft, heather grey. When did I learn
to recognize colors like heather grey?

There is nothing to inspire excitement, or
coax open damp thighs. He is what I hope
has happened to the boys who used to tease me
about my glasses back in school. This is what
you see when you finally turn my way,
my face a mere spring board propelling
your eyes on to the next co-ed, the next goth
girl, the next mall rat, and I wonder if
my heart will ever stop breaking over it.

Not a Poet

The art is still new
to his hands. There is nothing
beyond the relief, the swift
sound of church bells in
wind he hears when
he puts pencil to paper, when
he can see the equation of
his words add up to a stanza.
He is not a poet, yet
he compares himself to Wordsworth
as he tries to capture the clouds
in his loose leaf notebook
with an abundance of adjectives and
poor comparisons between their movement
and the way marshmallows melt,
turning to mush.

Fission

I have always chosen corners over crowds,
always slid to a squat on the floor, hunched
my shoulders, and wrapped my arms over my head.
I have always given the world my back.

I am not surprised to find myself living in
a 14 x 17 studio apartment wallpapered in books
from floor to ceiling, wobbly stacks full of zombies,
witches, and sleeping dragons I must

tip toe through just to reach the bathroom.
Some days I wish I had a sword.
I have gently encouraged my phone to stop
ringing. The less attention I pay it

the quieter it gets, until there is nothing
but the peculiar silence of the North Bronx,
the hissing of two cats fighting below
my window, possums tearing through

garbage bags down by the curb.
I wish I could be shocked by how deliberately
I have shrunk my world, reduced it to a single cell
and made myself the nucleus, but I have known

from the first time my friends turned theirs backs
on me at recess, to the last time my boss dressed
me down for a mistake she made, this was coming
as surely as a mushroom cloud.

How the Story Ends

If we build it, they will come
because everybody knows
fire is the only thing that can
bring New York City to its knees.

We'll start with a couple pieces
of rotted-out wood from the
Battery Park City Pier and some
nail-driven two-by-fours struck
from the set of the most recently
shuttered Broadway show.

We'll take them to Times Square,
to the pedestrian walkways
that used to be traffic lanes,
strike a match, and give the tourists
a reason to raise their cameras.

It will start small, a flower bud not quite
in bloom. More likely to consume itself
than the kindling. But it will eventually
get hungry and begin to feed. We'll
drop reams of printer paper into its mouth
and it will grow ravenous.

We'll toss in the office coffee maker,
hear it sizzle and pop, and do a war
dace around the pyre. A woman
in a red dress will throw in her
day planner, and some bum, his

"spare dime" sign. And when
the Police come, we'll just invite
them to throw in their uniforms.
We'll ward off the men from
Engine 65 with s'mores and
camp fire stories The fire will grow

until plumes of black smoke
swallow up the sky scrapers, and
paint soot across all the corporate
office windows. The Executive VPs
will storm the streets commanding

everyone to get back to work, but for once
we won't let them decide how the story
ends. We will lead them into the bonfire
to the sound of Martha and the Vandellas
"Dancing in the Streets." We will dance
because we own this town.

What Remains

Some say the house was torn down, and some say
it was never built. One tale goes that a band of Gypsies
looted the place, stripping it first of jewelry
and change purses, then end tables, wall hangings,
and finally shingles and floorboards, leaving nothing
but a set of concrete steps in the sand, rising up to a porch
that wasn't there, man's best friend waiting patiently
at the foot to be called in for supper. The Grandmothers
said he was never a puppy. As they moved from dolls
to lipstick to diamond rings, the mutt stayed the same,
forever panting his long pink tongue over mucus-yellow
canines, enduring heat waves, downpours,
and sand storms without howl or complaint. He remains
as devoted to those stairs as the Sphinx to the Great Pyramid,
devoted to the memory of climbing feet. Some say
the gypsies were so long without a meal
that they chopped off his left hind leg and made stew.
Others say his momma accidentally chewed it off
while severing the umbilical cord. All we know for sure is
if he were ever to walk, he would look the way sorrow feels.
Sometimes he'll move that stump back and forth,
as if trying to scratch an itch, start slow
and then speed up, his haunch flapping helplessly,
the itch unrelieved.

Ain't Stoppin'

The doors close with their familiar electronic
bloomp-bloomp and the Seventh Avenue Express
2 Train lurches out of the 72nd Street subway station,
accelerating slowly at first, then faster until all of us
strap-hangers are swaying with the thump-bump
of each sharp turn and patch of uneven track.

We sail past 66th Street, home of the Lincoln Center
of Performing Arts. The place every ballerina in the city
thinks she is going, the back wall every opera singer
hopes his voice will reach. Where all the Juilliard and
"Fame" High School students go to study Shakespeare,
but we ain't stoppin' for them.

We go past 59th Street where the Time Warner
Building boasts the only twin towers left in Manhattan,
flying the flags of capitalism from their boxy
crowns. Even Christopher Columbus salutes
from his perch atop the roundabout named after him.
We sure as Hell ain't stoppin' for them.

Past 50th Street, the theatre district, all the glittering
marquees advertising musicals based on movies
based on books. Clumps of tourists who deserve
every shoulder check and elbow to the ribs they get
for blocking foot traffic, gazing up at the lights, the
windows, the sky scrapers, the black sky void of stars.
Nope, we ain't stoppin' for them.

We stop at Times Square, 42nd Street because
you got to pick up passengers at the Crossroads
of the World, and we let passengers off at
34th Street, Penn Station because we have to
get all the bridge and tunnel trash, with their big
hair and bigger mouths out of our City
and back to the 'burbs where they belong.

We pass 28th and 23rd Streets, Chelsea, where
all the starving artists migrated and opened galleries
once gentrification drove up the rents in SoHo.
And now there's an Olive Garden where there
was once an open air parking lot, and renting a
closet in the Chelsea Hotel starts at $2,000 a month,
more than any of today's Sid and Nancys can afford.
We ain't stoppin'.

We stop at 14th Street because there is always
room for a Greenwich Village freak or two, a beatnik
wannabe, a boy with a rainbow cape draped across
his slim shoulders, or a folk singer and her beat up
guitar case. Always room for a dream because
that's what this town is made of.

We sail on past Houston and Canal Streets, past
boutiques selling distressed jeans for $350 a pop,
and women are required to carry pooches in their
purses. Where I would get off if I wanted to go see
that indie film everyone is talking about at the
TriBeCa Film Festival, but New York's got more than
enough culture to go around so we ain't stoppin'.

I get off at Chambers Street because Brooklyn ain't
my thing. Too many hipsters sweating irony out there.
Transfer to the Downtown Local 1 train. We blow past
Cortlandt Street because buildings weren't the only things
to collapse that day. I stay in my seat as we pull into
the Rector Street station because what business would
a poet have in the Financial District?

Ride down to South Ferry, the end of the line,
and climb out into a day so bright the Hudson River
looks like a diamond mine. No wonder
they used to say the streets in America were paved
with gold. I bet Lady Liberty still believes it.
A line of people snakes through Battery Park
waiting to board a boat bound for Ellis Island.

All but one of my grandparents came over
"on the boat," their names carved onto the
American Immigrant Wall of Honor along with
those of over 700,000 others who passed through
on their way to a new life. On their way to
sweat shops and tenements, religious freedom and
political asylum. On their way off the boat. The line
to Ellis Island is long. This is where we stop.

Carla Criscuolo was born and raised in New York City. She holds an MFA in Creative Writing from the Vermont College of Fine Arts, and a BA in Creative Writing from Knox College. Her poetry has appeared in numerous literary magazines, including *Main Street Rag, South Jersey Underground, Boston Literary Magazine, decomp,* and *Amarillo Bay*. She currently lives on Long Island.

www.ingramcontent.com/pod-product-compliance
Lightning Source LLC
LaVergne TN
LVHW091234080426
835509LV00009B/1273